God's Paintbrush

by

Sandy Eisenberg Sasso

author of In God's Name *and*
Noah's Wife: The Story of Naamah

illustrated by

Annette Compton

Dedication and Acknowledgments

Sandy Eisenberg Sasso

To my children, Debora and David, the colors in my paintbox.

This book was first conceived in a class taught by Dr. Nelle Slater. My gratitude for her encouragement and the freedom she gave me to explore this idea. My thanks to Stuart Matlins, Jevin Eagle and Rachel Kahn, who believe in the religious imagination of children and who helped make publishing this book a delight. To Mary K. Cauley, my thanks for her patient typing and retyping of this manuscript and to Susan Cohen, my appreciation for her advice and support. To my editor, Virginia Koeth, I am indebted for her keen sense of style and clarity.

To see one's words come alive by an artist's hand is to receive a special gift. Annette Compton has surely painted with God's paintbrush.

For my husband, Dennis C. Sasso, I am forever grateful. His sharp eye, gentle hand and enduring faith are in this book. This book could not have been written without the love of my father, Israel Eisenberg, whose memory is for a blessing, and my mother, Freda Eisenberg. They gave me the canvas upon which I first began to paint.

Annette Compton

The illustrations are dedicated to a Power greater than myself,
to Raymond and Patricia for the gift of creativity in creating me,
and to Gordon Haines Taylor for the patience and love to witness the paintbrush at work.

Special 10th Anniversary Edition © 2004
Text © 1992 and 2004 by Sandy Eisenberg Sasso
Illustrations © 1992 by Jewish Lights Publishing

The Library of Congress has cataloged the original hardcover edition as follows:
Sasso, Sandy Eisenberg.
God's paintbrush/Sandy Eisenberg Sasso: with illustrations by Annette Compton.
p. cm.
Summary: Discusses God's place in the universe and how God touches our world.
ISBN 1-879045-22-2 (First edition)
10 9 8 7 6 5 4 3 2 1
1. God—Juvenile literature. [1. God] I. Compton, Annette, 1959– ill. II. Title.
BL473.S27 1992   211.—dc20   92-15493

Special 10th Anniversary Edition ISBN 1-58023-195-0

JEWISH LIGHTS Publishing, a division of LongHill Partners, Inc.
Sunset Farm Offices, Route 4, P.O. Box 237, Woodstock, Vermont 05091
Tel: (802) 457-4000   Fax: (802) 457-4004   www.jewishlights.com

Printed in Singapore

Sometimes I think the clouds are made
of white balls of cotton yarn,
God's way of painting pictures in the sky.

And then, a big wind comes
and blows the pictures away—
like a giant eraser.

A sunbeam peeked in my window this morning, and painted a rainbow on my wall.

I think the sunbeam is God's paintbrush dipped in a watercolor sea, painting clouds and coloring our world.

What color would you paint the world today?

Sometimes I imagine that
when it gets very dark at night,
the flowers, trees, mountains
and oceans are afraid.

I wonder if God made
the stars for them
to go to bed with
and the moon
to be their night light?

When are you afraid?

What makes you feel better?

5

Sometimes when the clouds look grey and dark,
I think they are angry or sad.
And the rain, I think, is God's tears.

Sometimes the oceans make giant waves with white foam on the top.
I imagine that pleases God, and God laughs.

When the fizz on my favorite ice cream soda tickles my nose, it makes me laugh. Maybe it makes God laugh, too.

What makes you cry and laugh?

What do you think would make God cry or laugh?

Yesterday our class played kickball.
I fell while running to first base and
scraped my knee.
    It hurt.
    The school nurse put a bandage
over the scrape.
    In a few days, it was all better.

Last month my best friend had to move away.
    I was sad.
    I hurt inside.
My Dad said we can visit in the summer
and we can write letters or call on the
telephone when we miss each other a lot.

What Dad said made me feel better.
But when I think of my best friend,
far away, I still hurt a little.

I wonder if God hurts and what might help
God feel better.
    Maybe I could be God's friend.

What do you think makes God hurt?

How can you be God's friend?

9

My class went on a hike the other day.
We climbed to the top of a mountain,
and I shouted H - E - L - L - O!
I heard a voice call back
      H - E - L - L - O!
It sounded just like my voice—
only far away.

My teacher said, the sound I heard
was an echo.
It was fun to hear our own voices—
we kept calling out, and the sound
from space kept calling back.

I wonder what God's voice sounds like.
      Is it deep and gruff?
      Is it soft and gentle?
      Is it loud or quiet?
I think, God keeps calling out and maybe
we are the sound that calls back.
      Maybe people are God's echo.

How are you God's echo?

What does God call us to do?

My Mom and I went shopping in the city.
There in the middle of a crowded
department store was a little boy.
	He was alone and crying.
	My Mom held his hands in hers and
took him to a clerk who worked at the store.
The clerk made an announcement over the
loud speaker saying that a little boy was lost.

Before long, his mom came and gave him a
great big hug. My Mom hugged me, too.
I'm not sure why.

One of the things I like about my Mom is her
hands. When I was just a baby, my Mom says
her hands rocked the cradle, so I wouldn't cry.
	I wonder if God's hands rock the world.

How can your hands help God's hands?

I have lots of things that belong to me.
They're mine, and I don't like anyone
messing with them.

Sometimes I think God belongs to me.
When I'm surprised or frightened,
I say, "My God!"
But then I think,
no one can own God.
God doesn't belong to anyone.
We belong to God.

*Are there times when you feel like
you don't belong?*

I wonder if God has a big lap to curl up in,
just like my Mom's, and strong arms, just like Dad's,
to lift me up and catch me when I fall.

I wonder if God has strong hands
to hold me tight, just like Mom's, and big shoulders,
just like Dad's, to carry me when I am tired.

What makes you feel safe and warm and loved?

Sometimes I like to play
hide and seek with my friends.
We count to ten
and then start looking.
But today my friends
got tired of looking,
and went away before
they found me.
    I felt very lonely.

On Monday, I broke my Mom's vase.
I was scared.
I hid behind the large sofa
in our living room.
Mom came home.
I was glad when she found me.
    I felt lonely all by myself.

Sometimes I think God hides,
and we don't want to look for God,
because we are too busy or too afraid.

    God must feel
    terribly lonely then, too.

Where would you look for God?

15

When the wind blows warm, making grass, trees and flowers dance, it makes my hair brush against my face.

I think the wind is God's breath moving through the world, making it come alive.

I think that God's breath moves through me, too.

That makes me special,
    having a little bit of God inside me.
That makes everyone special,
    having God's breath inside them.

We can make words and music with God's breath.

What kind of words and music does God's breath make?

Walking home this afternoon,
I heard the wind whistle,
    a dog bark,
    a bird chirp,
    a baby cry.

All these sounds—
    some soft,
    some loud.
They are God's song.

If you sang a song to God, what would you sing?

When I go to bed at night, I sleep on cool cotton sheets.
I hold a soft furry teddy bear—very close.

My Mom gives me a big kiss, and her cheeks feel warm and soft.
My Dad gives me a big hug, and his face feels scratchy, but good.
All these good feelings, I think, are God's touch.

What does God's touch feel like to you? How can you help God touch the world?

The world revolves around the sun.
The planets spin far out in space.
Stars sparkle and meteors shoot light through the sky.

I think they are God's dance,
God's way of keeping the world turning.

When I help a friend,
when I make someone smile,
I think I am part of God's dance.

Can you dance God's dance?

What would it look like?

21

My tooth fell out last night.
My parents said that it was in order
to make room for my new one.
I didn't really like losing it,
even though I found a dollar
under my pillow in its place.

I wonder if the trees mind losing their leaves
in the fall or if the snow minds
when it melts to make room for spring.

I think God paints the leaves
bright colors in the fall,
and makes the sun warm in spring,
because God likes changes.
      God likes the world to grow.
.
How are you changing?

How are you growing?

Sometimes I think God is just like my Dad
when he holds the back seat of my new two-wheel bicycle
just long enough for me to catch my balance.
Then he lets go, and I ride all by myself!
But it's nice to know he's running right alongside me.

Sometimes I think God is just like my Mom
when she helps me look both ways in crossing the street
and then lets me go—all by myself!
But it's nice to know she's still watching me at the corner.

*What makes you feel big enough to do something,
all by yourself, for the very first time?*

My friend is great at math.
She always gets 100 on her tests.
My brother is captain of his baseball team.
He always gets home runs.

Sometimes when I get lots of red X's
all over my math paper,
I think I'd like to be just like my friend.

When I get up to bat and strike out,
I think I'd like to be just like my brother.

But then I think,
    I enjoy gymnastics.
    I can do one-handed
    cartwheels!
    I am glad to be me!

Perhaps God gave each of us
a special gift that makes us
different from anyone else,
and when we share that gift—
    God is happy.

What is your gift?

How do you share your gift?

27

Today our school went for a hike.
The sky looked like a lemon meringue pie.
The fields of flowers seemed like layers
of orange, red and purple jelly beans.

The vines looked just like a giant jump rope
and the hills like big slippery slides.
The branches of the trees
made a fantastic jungle gym.

I wonder if God likes lemon meringue pie
and jelly beans—just like me.

Sometimes my parents tell me
to eat more green vegetables
and fewer jelly beans!

Maybe they are right, but I still like
pink lemonade jelly beans the best.

I wonder if God likes to play.
Sometimes grown-ups don't want
to play because they are too busy
or too tired.
   I think that makes God sad.
   I think God likes me to play.

Who is in your favorite playground?

How do you play in God's playground?

In September, a new boy came to school.
During recess, nobody picked him
for the soccer team.
      At lunch, he ate all by himself.

What I remember most about him
were his eyes.
      They looked sad.

My teacher had us all do a mural one day.
The new boy helped me draw a lion.
He is a great artist.
      Maybe we will be friends.

My teacher watched
us working together.
What I remember most about
my teacher were her eyes.
      They looked happy.

THE ENVIRONMENT

I wonder if God has eyes.
If so, they must be just like my teacher's.
They see when people are sad or happy.

If you saw the world through God's eyes, what would you see?

Sometimes on a bright day
when I close my eyes real tight,
I see all kinds of colors—
green and purple and red and blue.
I think these are just like God's colors.

I know God's colors are in me, too.
And I can paint with God's paintbrush.